CONTENTS

T0068880

Notes from the original publication of French Suites

These six little Suites, to which, in the course of time, the by-name "French" was applied because they were written in the French style of that period (being similar to those by F. Couperin), are here presented in a new edition after an original MS., with emendations by J. S. Bach's own hand, said MS. having been found among F. W. Rust's literary remains. It contains, however, only the first four Suites, the fifth and sixth, added later to the series by Bach, owe most of their corrections to an old edition by M. Clementi.

On the whole, the style of these Suites is free, rather than scholastic, and they are of moderate technical difficulty. Their peculiarly attractive melodies are more prominent than in many other of the master's works. For these reasons, too, apart from their solid merit, they may rightly be regarded as belonging to that class of compositions which, in a sense, serve as agreeable recreative studies for proficient students. The above remarks are, however, chiefly applicable to the last three Suites.

French Suites
Thematic Index
Suite I

Suite II

Suite III

English Suites
Book I

Thematic Index

Suite I

PRÉLUDE

SARABANDE

BOURRÉE I

BOURRÉE II

GIGUE

ALLEMANDE

COURANTE I

COURANTE II *(with two Doubles)*

DOUBLE I

DOUBLE II

Suite II

PRÉLUDE

ALLEMANDE

COURANTE

GIGUE

SARABANDE *(avec les agréments)*

BOURRÉE I

BOURRÉE II

Suite III

PRÉLUDE

ALLEMANDE

COURANTE

GIGUE

SARABANDE *(avec les agréments)*

GAVOTTE I

GAVOTTE II *(Musette)*

English Suites
Book II

Thematic Index

French Suites
Suite I.

Johann Sebastian Bach
(1685–1750)

Allemande.

Andante con moto. (♩ = 72.)

Piano.

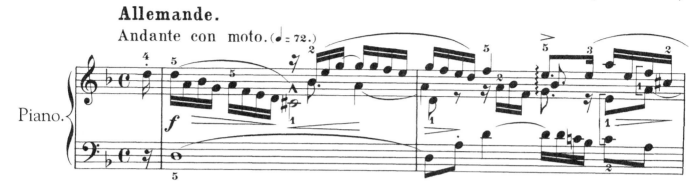

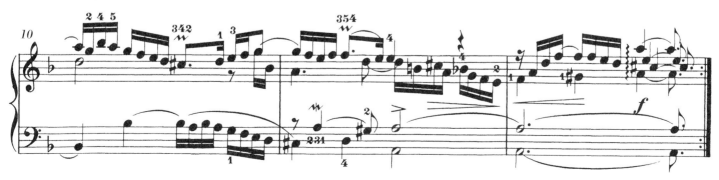

Courante.

Allegro. ($\bullet$ = 80.)

Sarabande.
Andantino. ($\bullet$ = 80.)

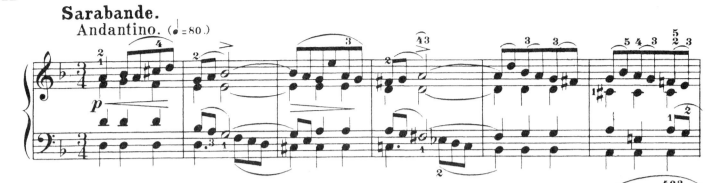

Menuet I.
Allegretto. ($\bullet$ = 116.)

Menuet II.

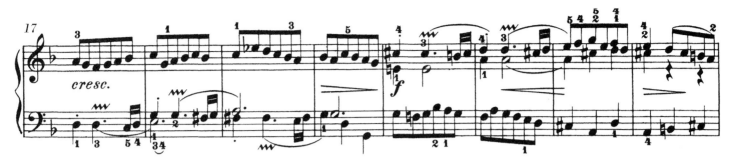

Gigue.

Allegro moderato e marcato. (♩ = 104.)

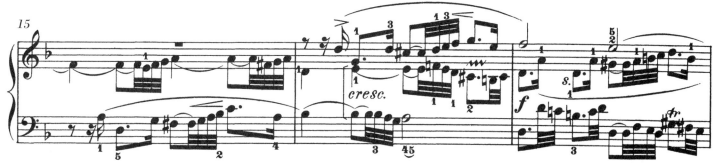

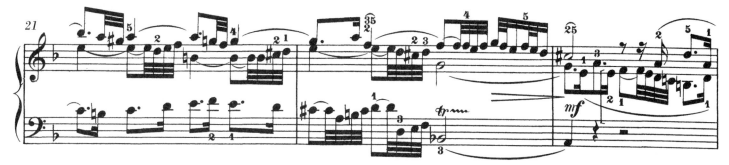

Suite II.

Allemande.
Allegro moderato. (♩ = 80)

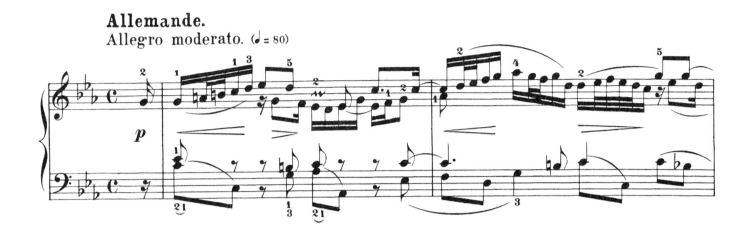

18

Courante.

Vivace. ($\dot{} = 76$)

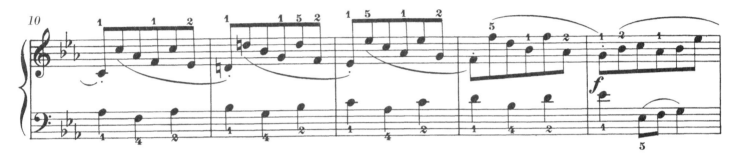

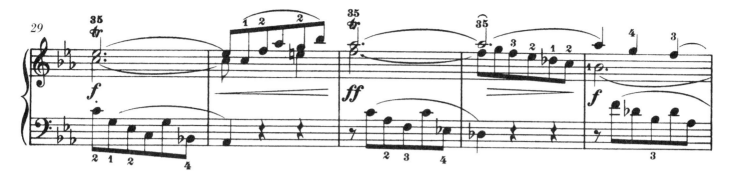

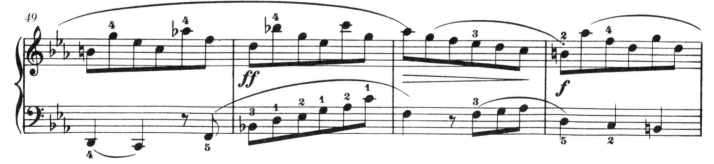

Sarabande.

Andantino. ($\bullet$ = 84.)

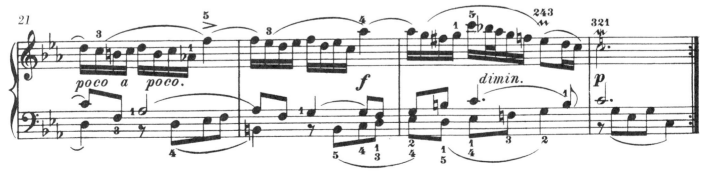

Air.
Un poco Andante. (♩ = 80)

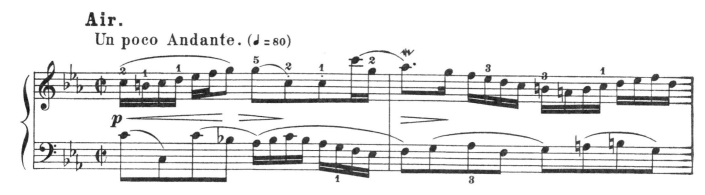

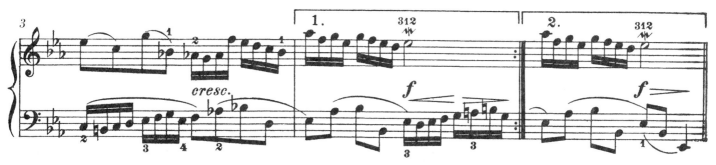

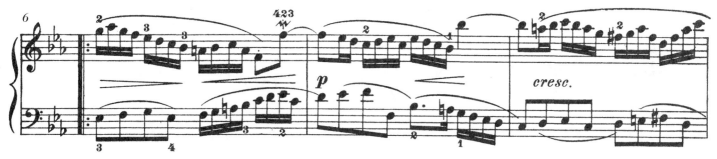

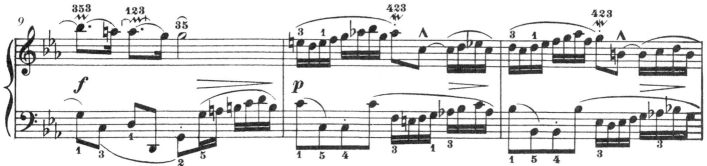

Menuet.

Allegretto. (♩ = 120)

Gigue.

Allegro. (♩. = 88)

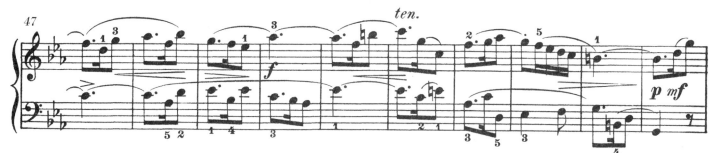

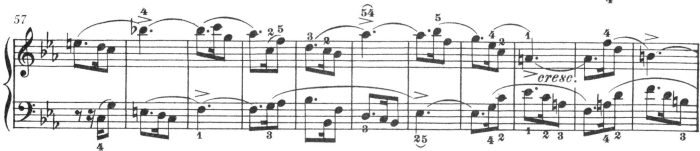

Suite III.

Allemande.

Allegro moderato.($\mathbf{\bullet}$=92)

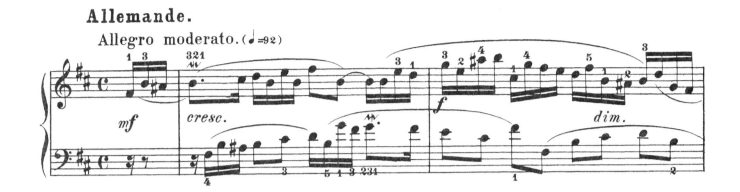

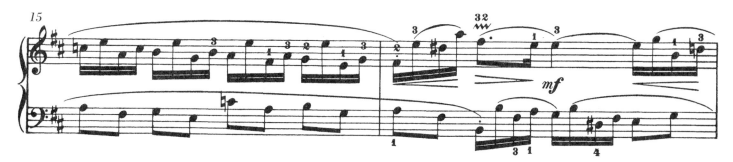

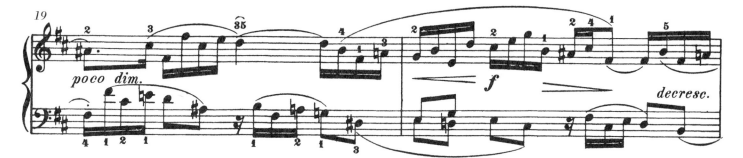

Courante.

Allegro vivace. ($\bullet$.=66.)

Sarabande.
Andantino.(♩=80)

Menuet I.

Con moto moderato.(♩=120)

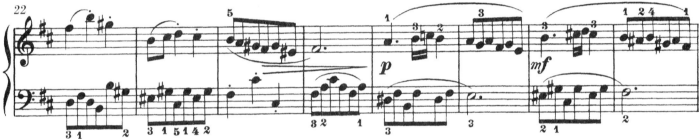

Menuet II.
(Trio.)

Men. I. da Capo.

Anglaise.

Vivace. (♩=104.)

Gigue.
Allegro. (♩.=84.)

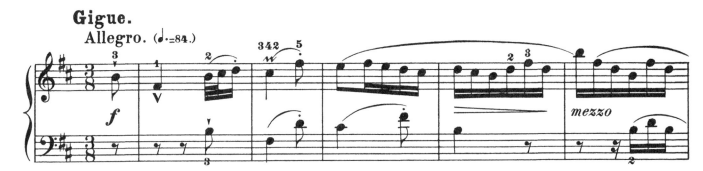

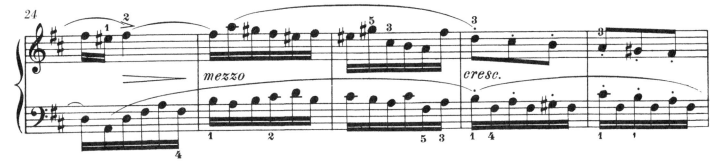

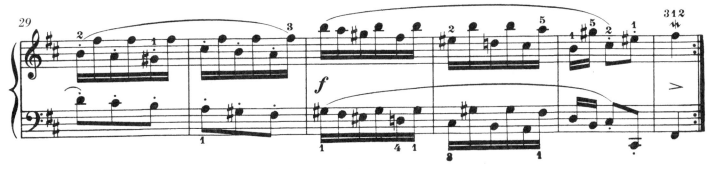

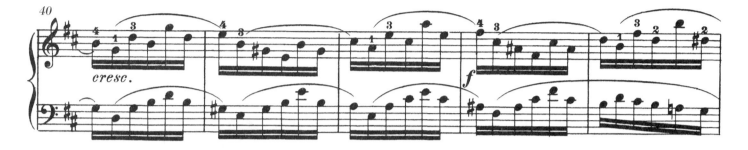

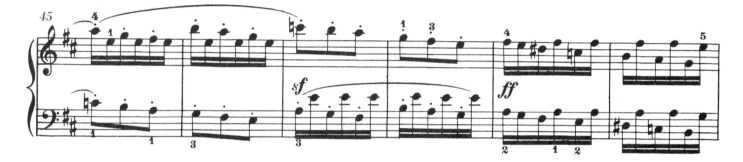

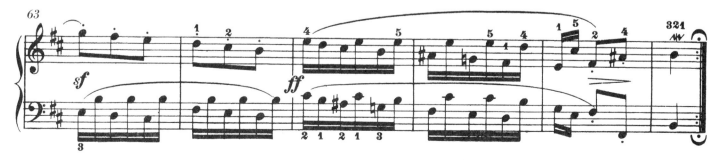

Suite IV.

Allemande.

Allegro moderato.($\bullet$ = 100)

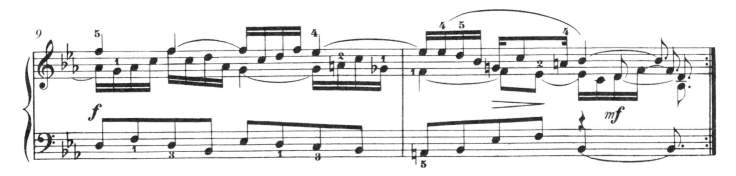

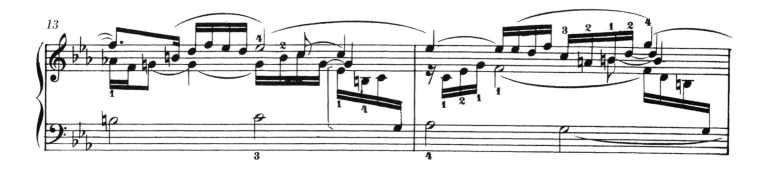

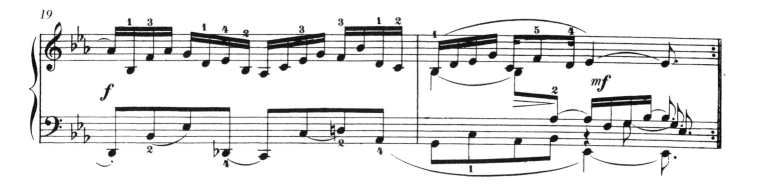

Courante.

Allegro. (♩ = 138)

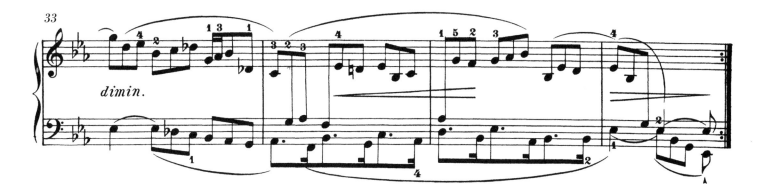

Sarabande.

Andantino. (♩ = 88)

Gavotte.

Scherzando. ($\flat$ = 96.)

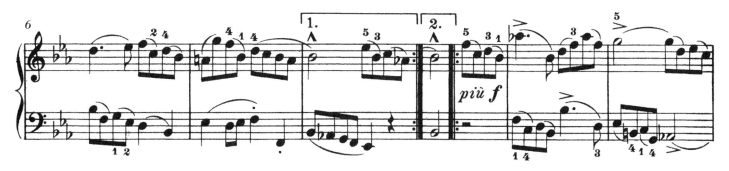

Menuet.

Tranquillo. ($\flat$ = 108.)

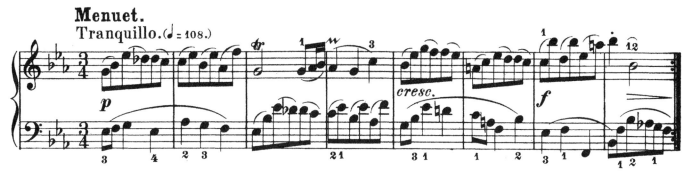

Air.

Un poco Allegro.(♩ = 104.)

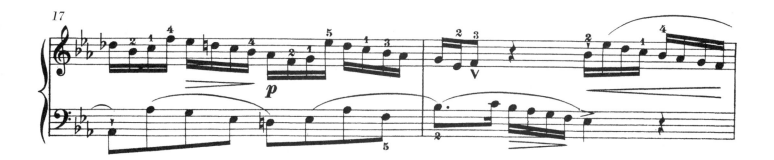

Gigue.
Allegro vivace.(♩.=120)

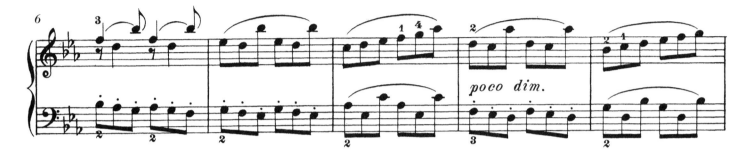

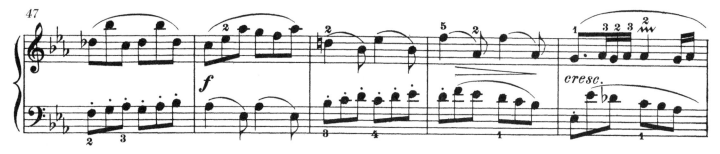

Suite V.

Allemande.
Allegretto. (♩ = 80.)

Courante.

Allegro. (♩=132.)

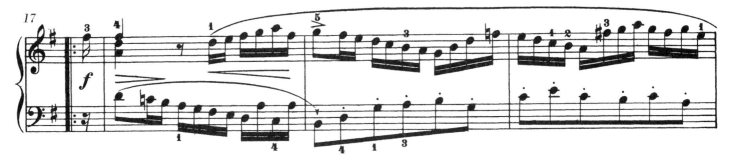

Sarabande.

Andante cantabile. (♩=84.)

Gavotte.

Un poco vivace. ($\quad = 88$)

Bourrée.

Allegro. ($\quad = 96$)

Loure.
Moderato. (♩ = 126)

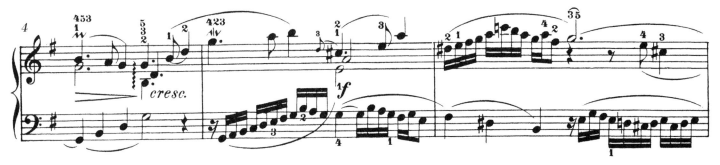

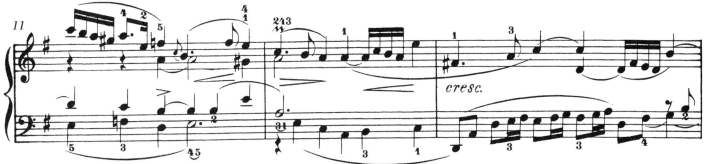

Gigue.
Vivace. (♩. = 76)

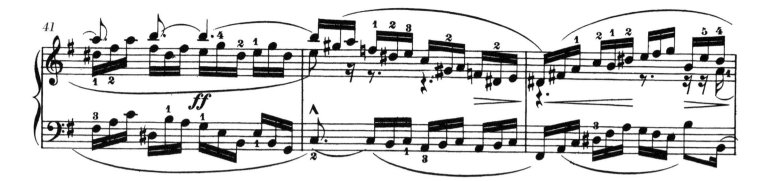

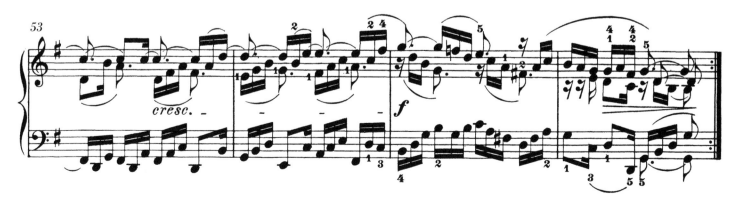

Suite VI.

Allemande.

Allegro moderato. (♩ = 92.)

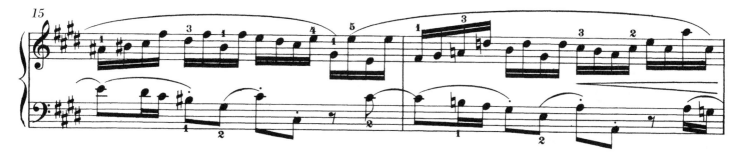

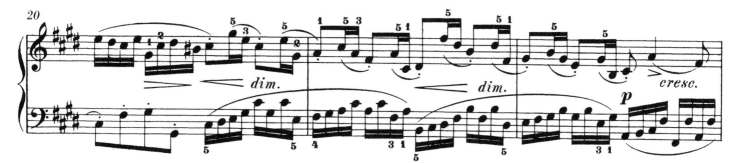

Courante.

Allegro e leggiero. (♩ = 138.)

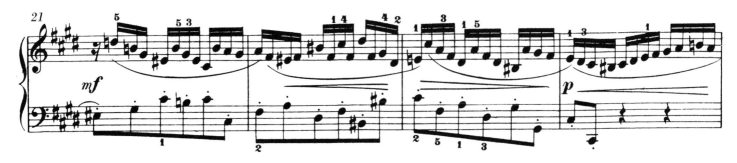

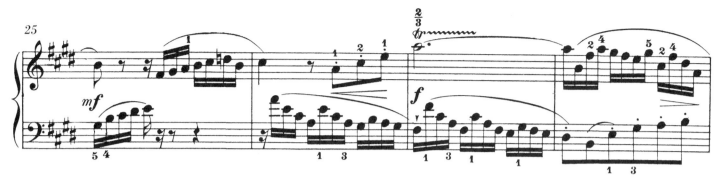

55

Sarabande.
Andante sostenuto. (♩=69.)

Gavotte.

Un poco vivace. ($\quad$=76.)

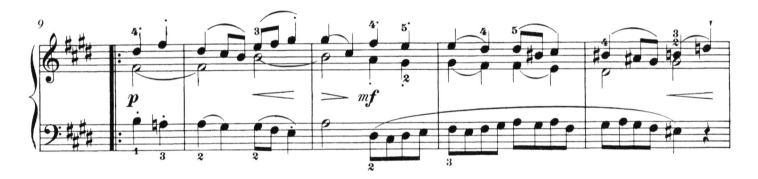

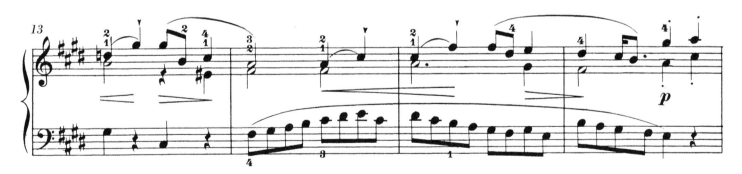

Polonaise.
Allegretto grazioso. (♩ = 100)

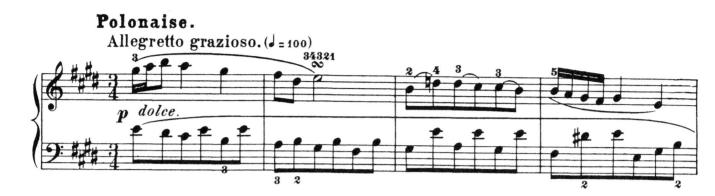

Bourrée.

Vivace. ($\quad = 112$)

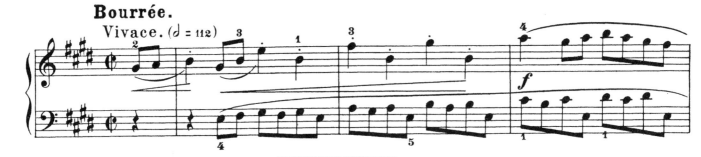

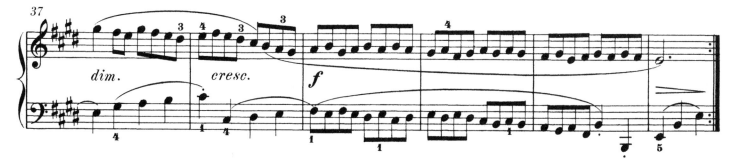

Menuet.

Moderato. (♩ = 120.)

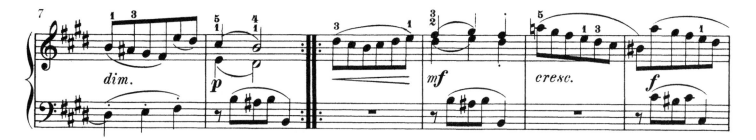

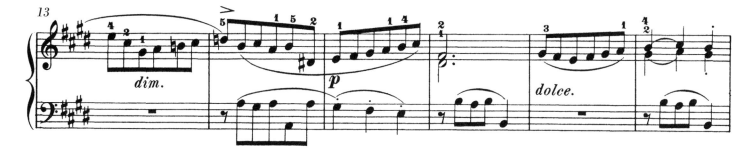

Gigue.

Molto Allegro. (♩.= 104.)

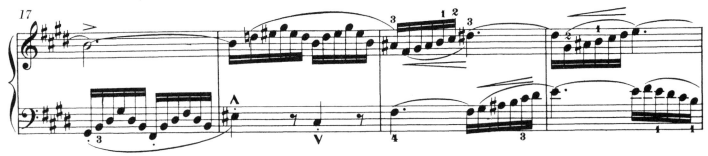

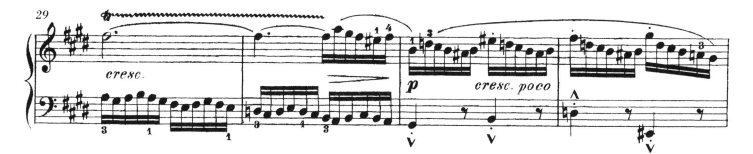

English Suites
Book I

Suite I.

Johann Sebastian Bach
(1685–1750)

Prelude.
Allegro. (♩.= 96.)

Piano.

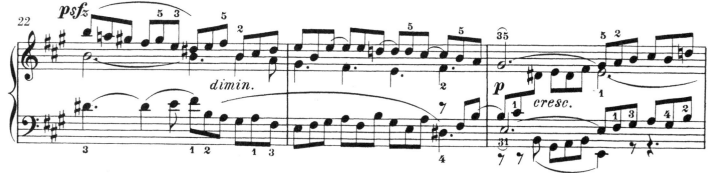

Allemande.

Allegretto moderato. (♩ = 72.)

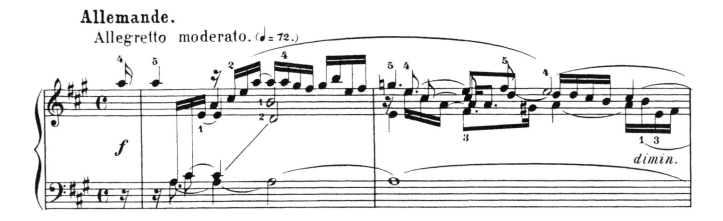

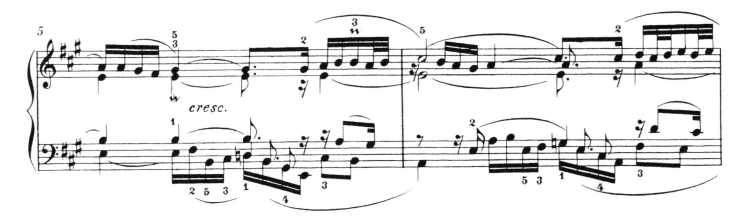

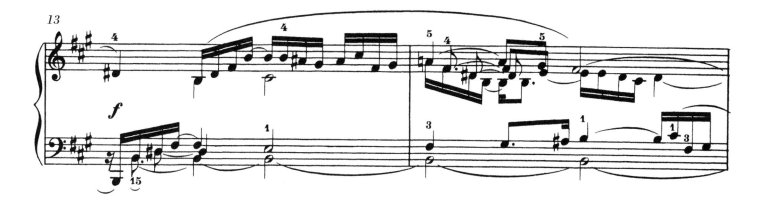

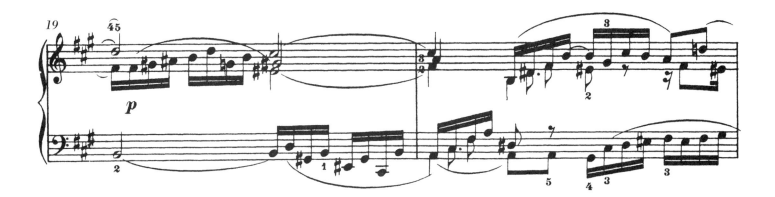

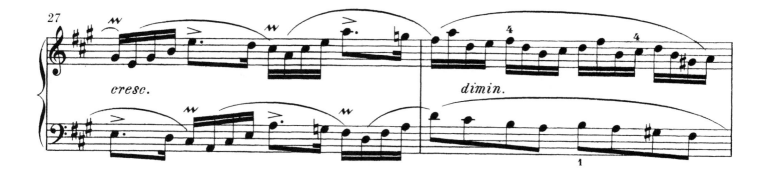

Courante I.

Allegro moderato. (♩ = 72.)

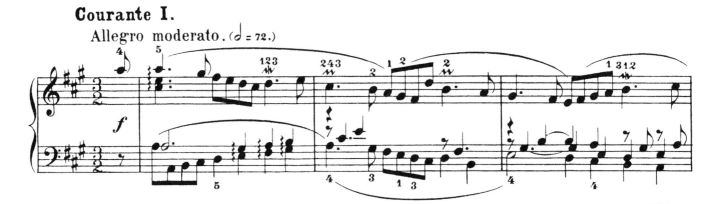

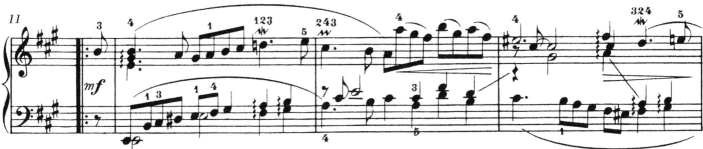

Courante II. (with two Doubles.)

Allegro moderato. (σ = 72.)

Double I.

Allegro moderato. ($\textit{d}$ = 72.)

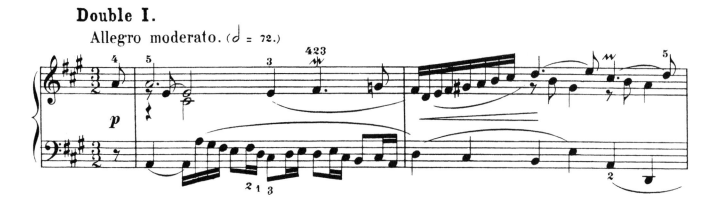

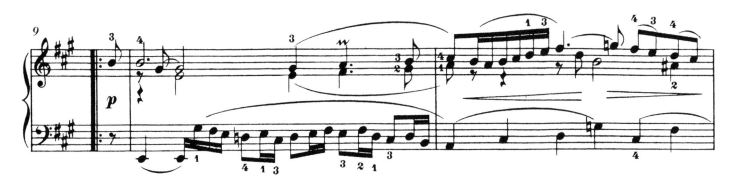

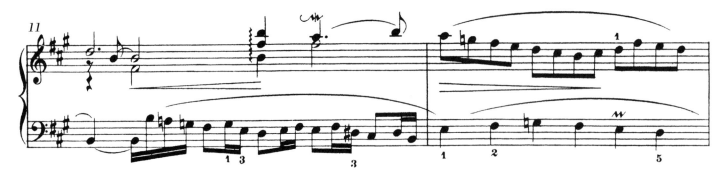

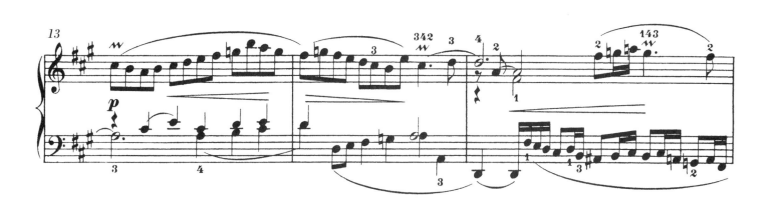

Double II.

Allegro moderato. (♩ = 72.)

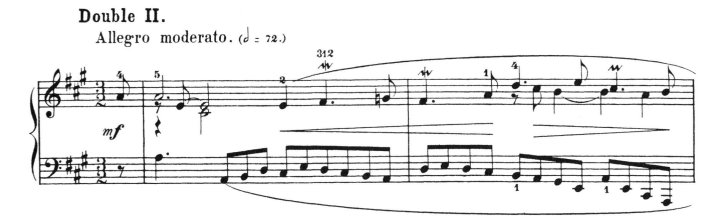

Sarabande.

Andante. (♩ = 60.)

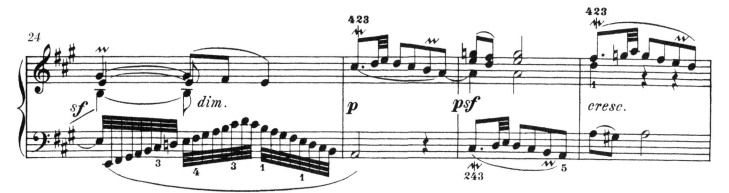

Bourrée I.
Molto allegro. ($\bf{\downarrow}$ = 100.)

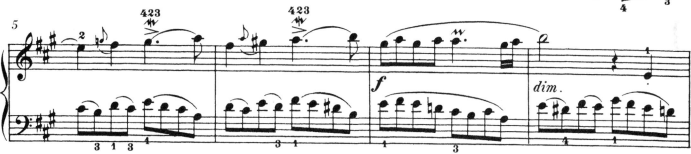

Bourrée II.

L'istesso tempo.

Bourrée I. D.C.

Gigue.

Allegro. ($\quad$ = 66)

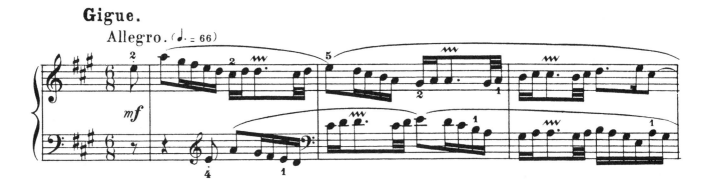

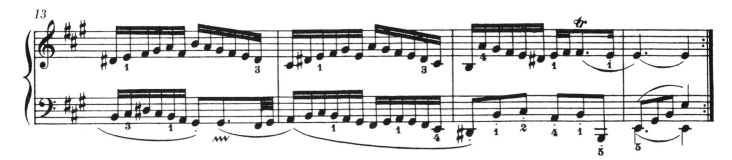

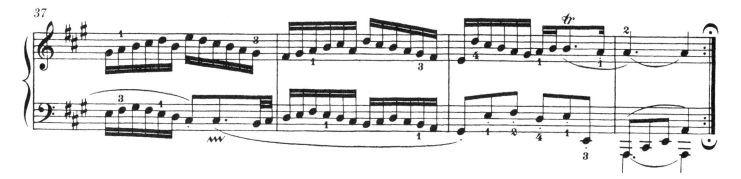

Suite II.

Prelude.
Allegro vivace. (♩ = 108)

Allemande.

Allegro moderato. (♩ = 92.)

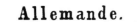
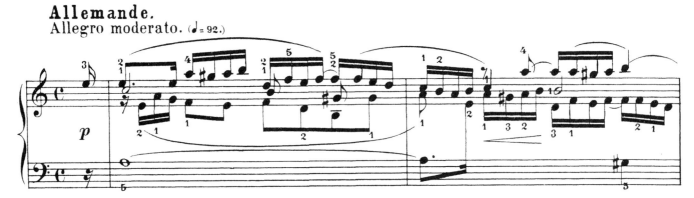

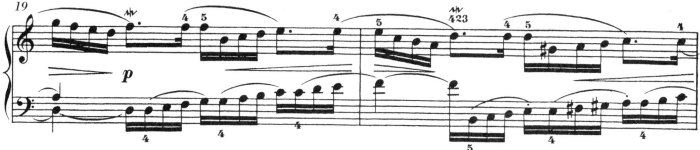

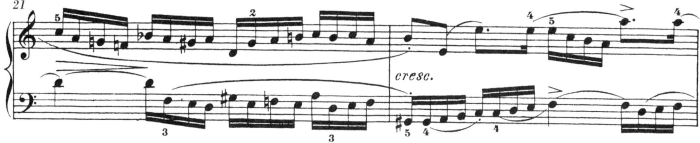

Courante.

Molto allegro. (♩= 96.)

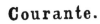

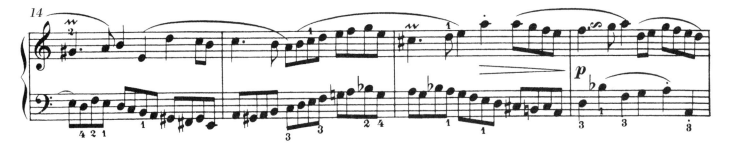

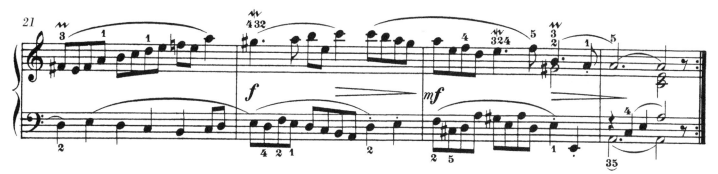

Sarabande.

Andante sostenuto. (♩=56.)

The ornaments (agréments) of the same Sarabande.

Bourrée I (alternatively.)

Molto allegro. (♩ = 100.)

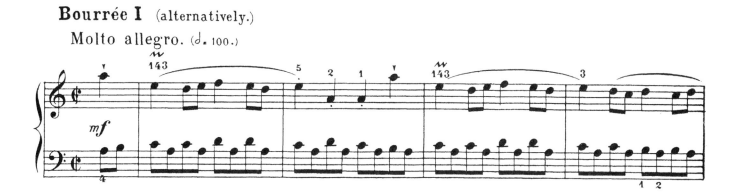

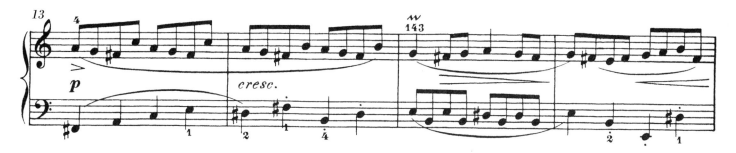

Bourrée II.

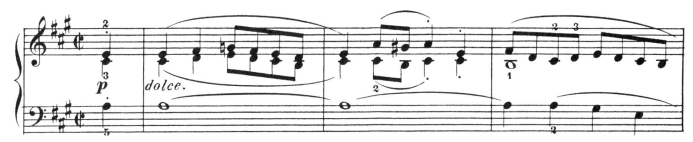

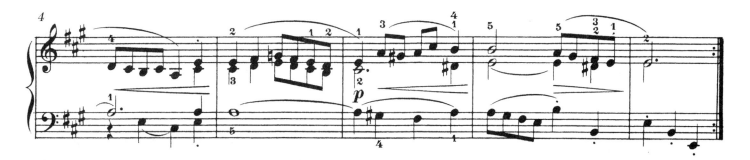

Bourrée I. D.C.

Gigue.

Presto. (♩. = 144)

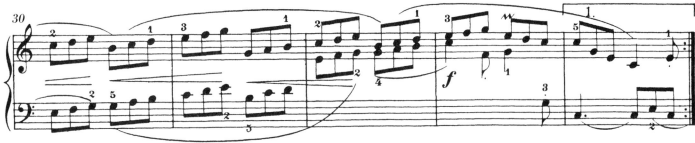

Suite III.

Prelude.

Allegro. (♩. = 76)

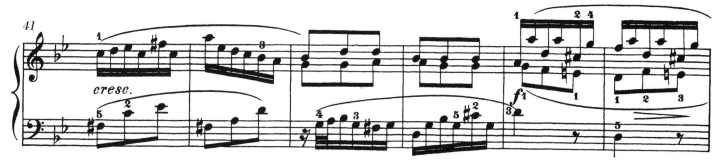

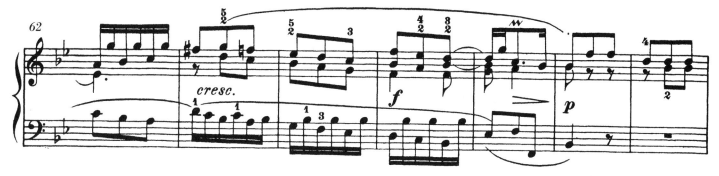

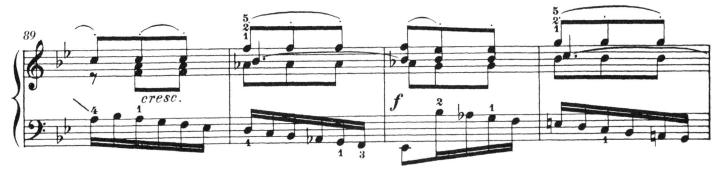

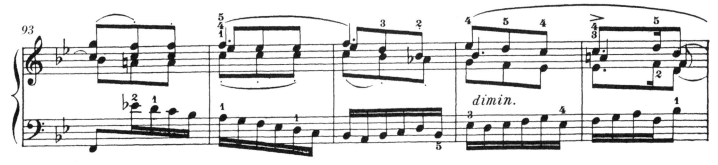

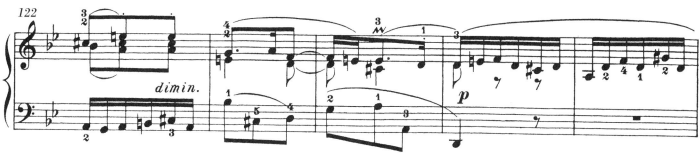

Allemande.

Allegro moderato. (♩ = 92)

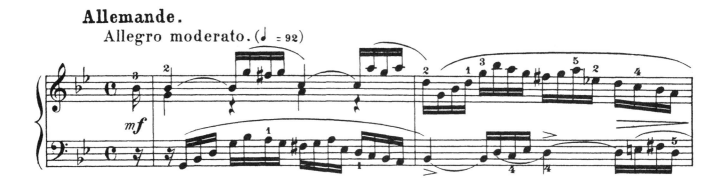

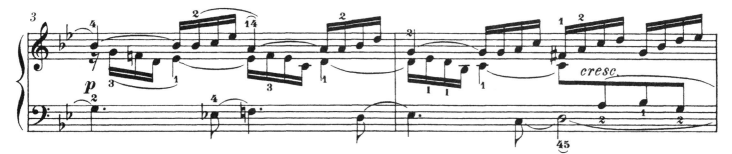

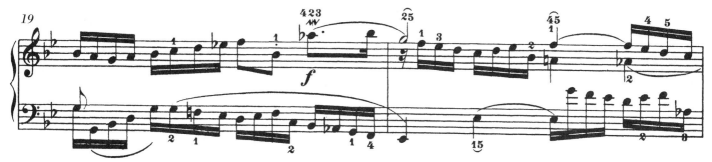

Courante.

Allegro vivace. ($\overset{.}{=}$84.)

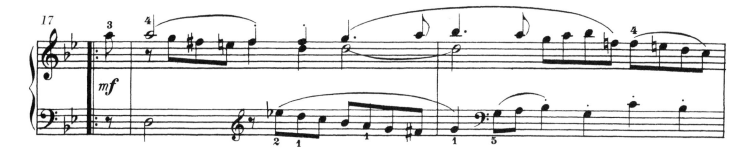

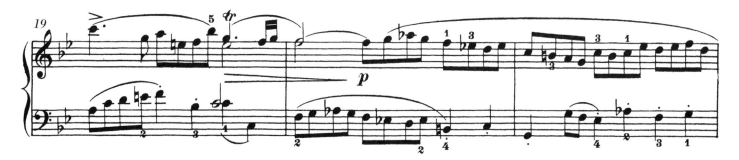

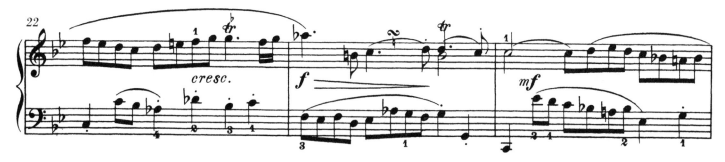

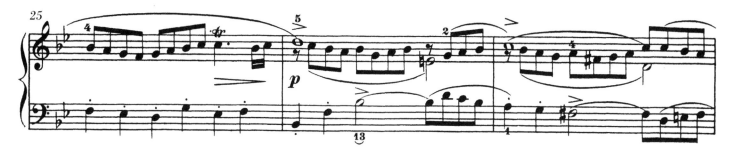

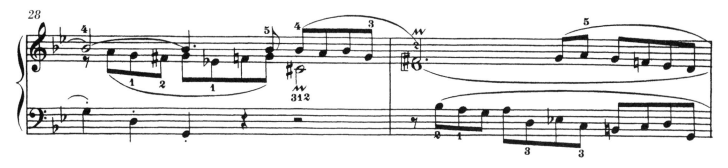

Sarabande.

Andante sostenuto. (♩=66.)

The ornaments (agréments) of the same Sarabande.

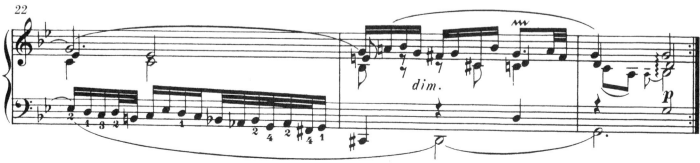

Gavotte I. (alternatively.)
Molto Allegro. (♩=100.)

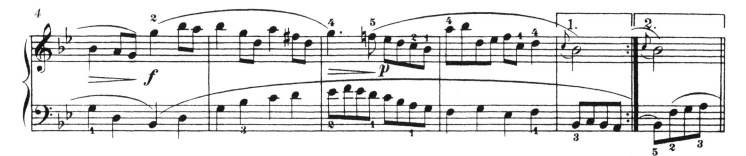

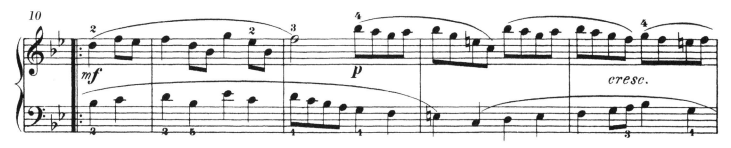

Gavotte II. (or the Musette.)
L'istesso tempo.

Gavotte I. Da Capo.

Gigue.

Molto Allegro. (♩. = 144.)

English Suites
Book II
Suite IV.

Johann Sebastian Bach
(1685–1750)

Prelude.

Allegro moderato.(♩ = 100)

Piano.

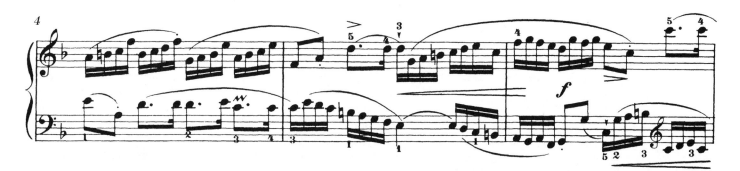

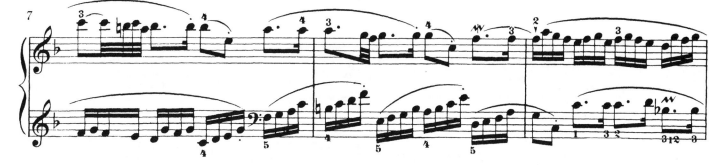

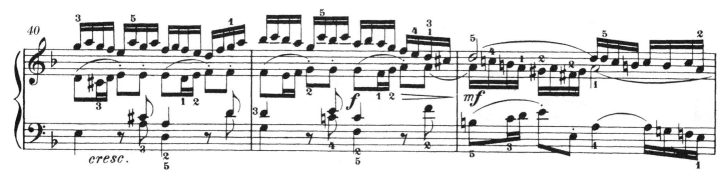

Allemande.

Allegro moderato. (♩ = 88)

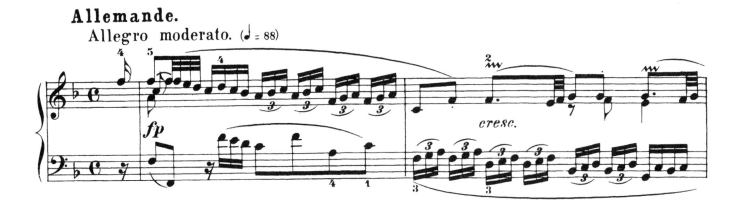

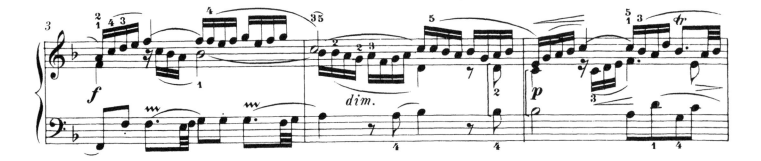

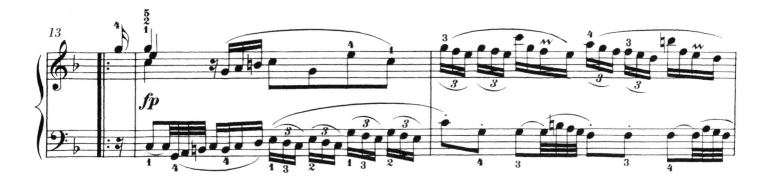

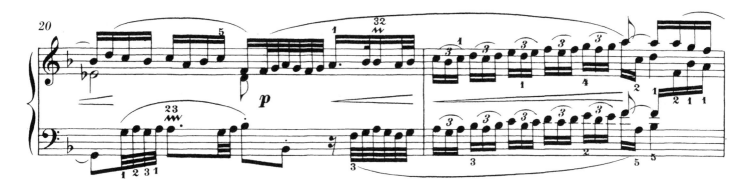

Courante.

Molto Allegro. (♩ = 96)

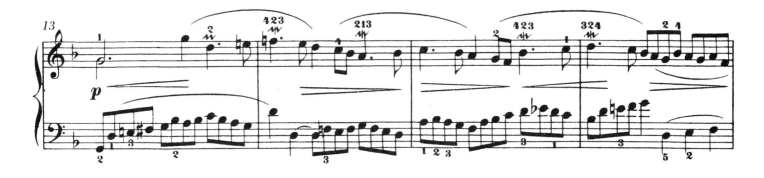

Sarabande.

Andante sostenuto. (♩=60)

Menuet I.

Andante con moto. (♩ = 116)

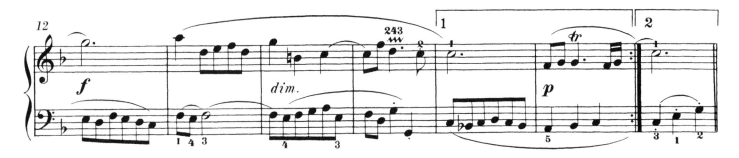

Menuet II.

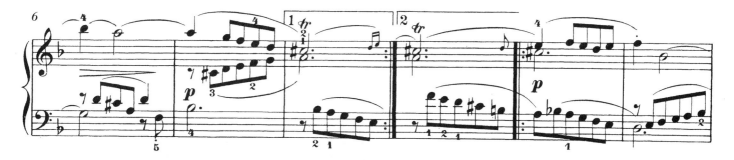

Menuet I D.C.

Suite V.

Prelude.
Allegro. (♩. = 72)

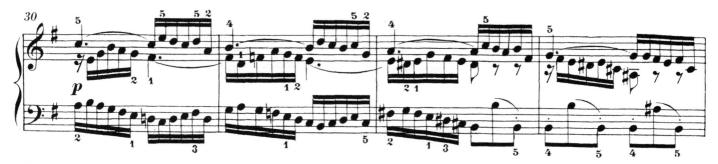

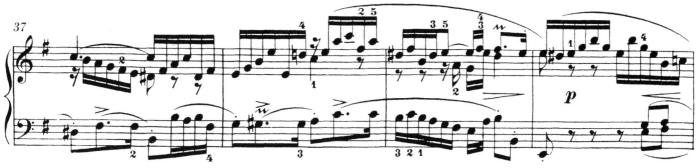

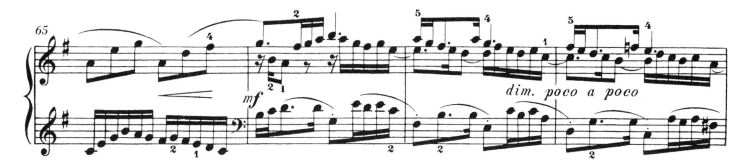

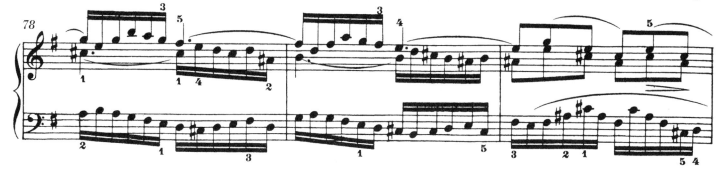

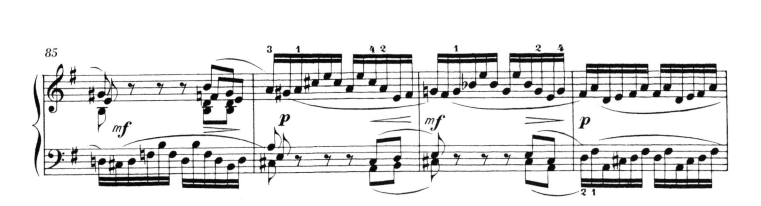

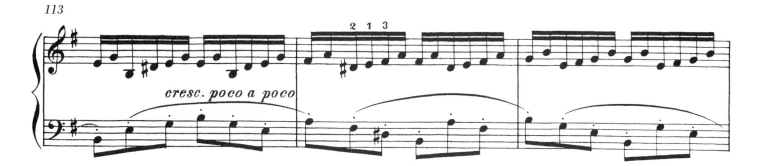

Allemande.

Allegro moderato. (♩ = 84)

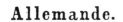

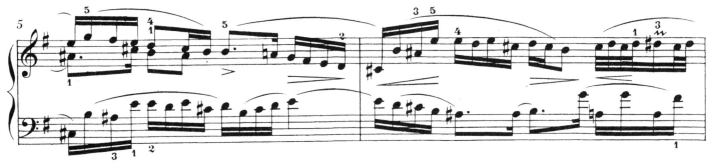

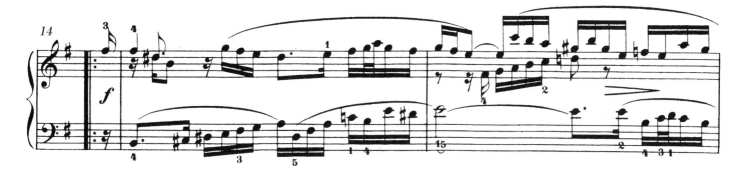

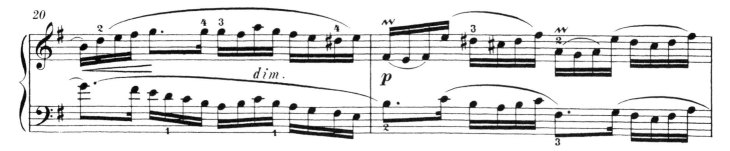

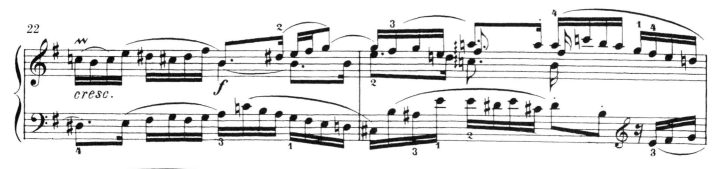

Courante.

Allegro vivace.($\textit{d}$ = 88)

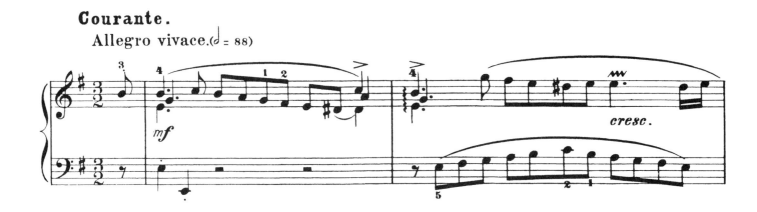

Sarabande.
Andante. (♩ = 63)

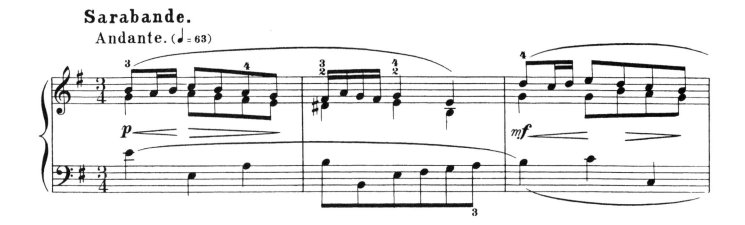

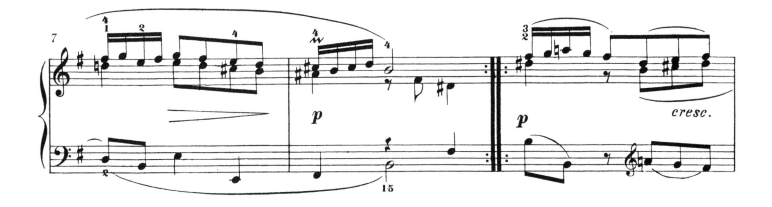

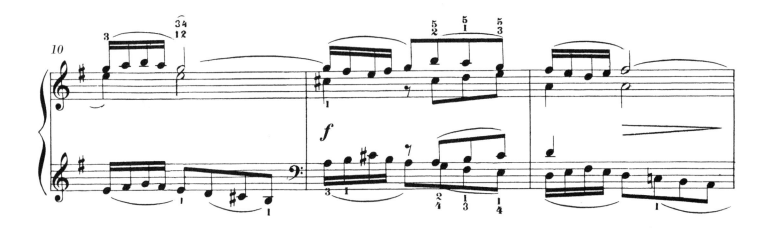

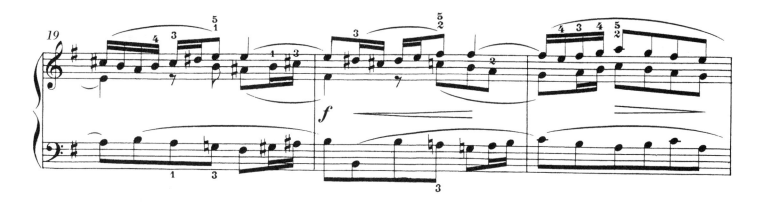

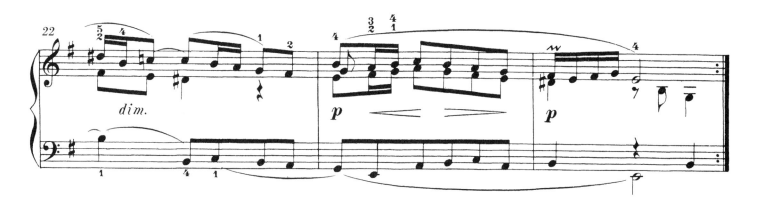

Passepied I.
(in Rondo-form.)

Allegretto vivace. (♩.= 66)

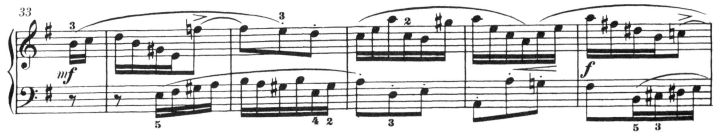

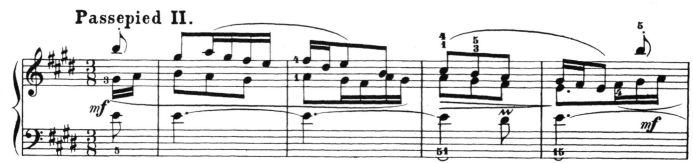

Passepied II.

Passepied I D.C.

Gigue.

Allegro. (♩. = 80)

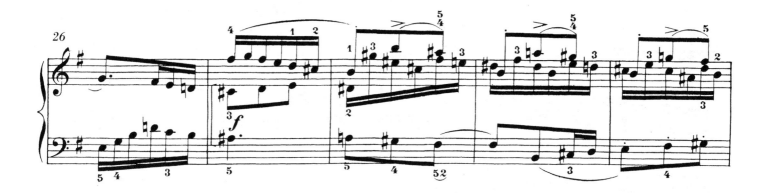

148

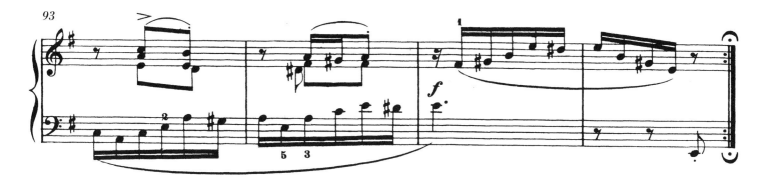

Suite VI.

Prelude.
Lento. ($\text{♩.} = 66$)

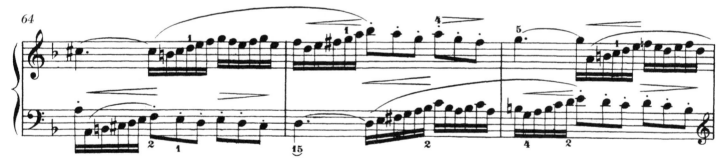

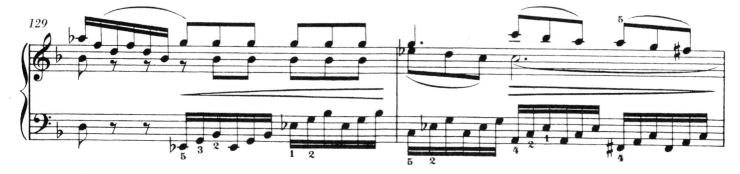

Allemande.

Lento moderato. (♩ = 76)

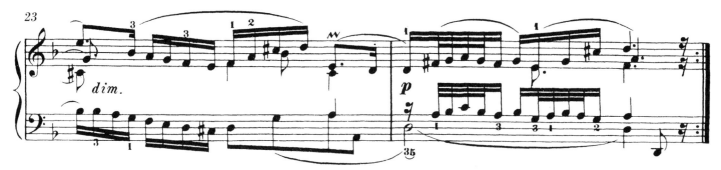

Courante.

Allegro vivace. ($\textit{d}$ = 92)

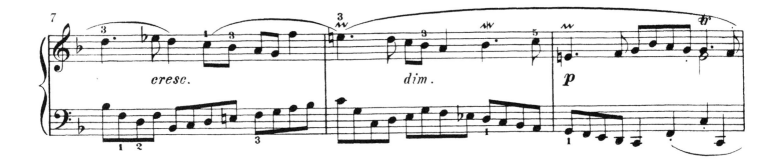

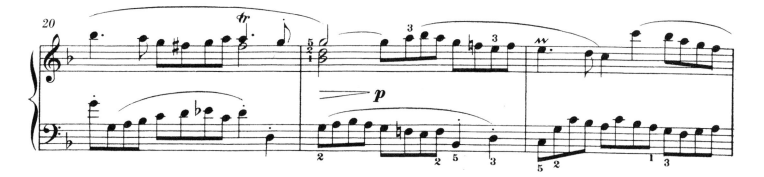

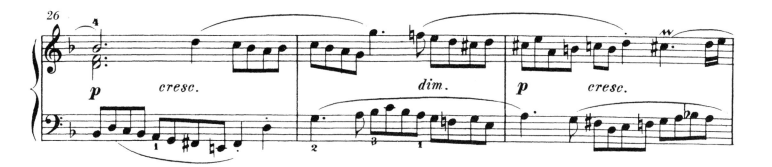

Sarabande.

Andante con moto. ($\bullet$=60)

Double.

Gavotte I.

Allegro vivace. ($\flat$ = 80)

il basso sempre legato.

Gavotte II.
(or the Musette.)

Gavotte I da capo.

Gigue.

Allegro. (♪ = 132)

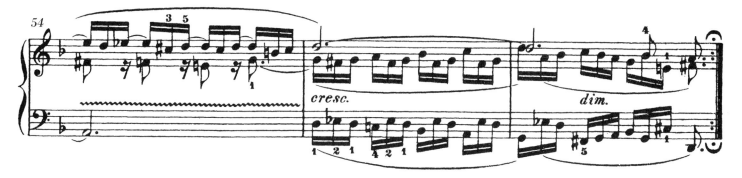